YOUR KNOWLEDGE HAS VALUE

Bibliographic information published by the German National Library:

The German National Library lists this publication in the National Bibliography; detailed bibliographic data are available on the Internet at http://dnb.dnb.de .

Imprint:

Copyright © 2016 GRIN Verlag
Print and binding: Books on Demand GmbH, Norderstedt Germany
ISBN: 9783668657397

This book at GRIN:

https://www.grin.com/document/415930

Samira Penner

Human Resource Management. Finding Talents

GRIN Verlag

GRIN - Your knowledge has value

Since its foundation in 1998, GRIN has specialized in publishing academic texts by students, college teachers and other academics as e-book and printed book. The website www.grin.com is an ideal platform for presenting term papers, final papers, scientific essays, dissertations and specialist books.

Visit us on the internet:

http://www.grin.com/

http://www.facebook.com/grincom

http://www.twitter.com/grin_com

FOM Hochschule für Oekonomie & Management

Studienzentrum Düsseldorf

Assignment

in the module

Human Resource Management

about the topic

Finding Talents

Author: Samira Penner

Date of submission: 2017-02-15

Table of Contents

List of Abbreviations

Cf.	Compare
Ed.	Editor
Eds.	Editors
EVP	Employee Value Proposition
F.	And the following page
Ff.	And the following pages
No.	Number
P.	Page
Vol.	Volume

List of Figures

1. Introduction

This first introductory chapter will provide the situational context through the problem description, present the central objectives and outline the general scope of work of the assignment.

1.1 Problem Description

Due to globalization and demographic changes, the context in which companies are operating has become more competitive and more complex. In fact, a new context has emerged, characterized by changes in the business environment including the market of potential candidates, which have led to the international challenge or "war for talent"[1], companies are facing today. Thus, there has been a transformation of the importance regarding the role and strategic management of talents within an organization which has meanwhile already become one of the top priorities in many companies. As a professional talent management can have a decisive influence on the future success and sustainability of an organization, many companies are seeking for suitable strategies and their operative implications to remain competitive.[2]

1.2 Objectives

The mentioned context presents the starting point for further analysis within the scope of this assignment. The objective is to present and analyse the three different theoretical talent management strategies of talent attraction, development and retention and find out, which operative implications they have for an organization in practice.

---

[1] Beechler, S., Woodward, I., The global "war for talent", 2009, p.373-285; Michaels, E., Handfield-Jones, H., Axelrod, B., The War for Talent, 2001, p.1.
[2] Cf. Eds. Heidelberger, M., Kornherr, L., Handbuch der Personalberatung, 2014, p.329f.; eds. Burton-Jones, A., Spender J., Human Capital, 2011, p.531ff.; eds. Scullion, H., Collings, D., Global Talent Management, 2011, p.3ff.; Hatum, A., Next Generation Talent Management, 2010, p.1f., 4-7; Collings, D., Mellahi, K., Strategic Talent Management, 2009, p.304-313; Guthridge, M., Komm, A., Lawson, E., Making talent a strategic priority, 2008, p.49-59; Barney, J., Firm Resources and Sustained Competitive Advantage, 1991, p.99-120.

1.3 Scope of Work

In order to provide the mentioned transfer from the theoretical analysis to the practical implications and answer the mentioned research question, the assignment follows a specific methodological and deductive approach. The logical line of thoughts implicates the formal structure of the assignment, which in detail is organized into four main chapters.

This introductory chapter is essentially a formal chapter which serves as a guideline to present the basic concept of the assignment through the problem description, objectives and scope of work.

The second chapter presents the theoretical foundation of the assignment by defining the terms and outlining the concept of talent and talent management as well as their importance within the context of the overall business strategy.

The third chapter focuses on the operative implications regarding the three major talent management strategies of talent attraction, development and retention in practice by presenting concrete activities and possible challenges to consider.

Eventually, the assignment is completed by the fourth and last chapter which again is a formal chapter to respond to the initially mentioned research question by providing a summary and conclusion of the essential findings of the assignment as well as a future outlook on the developments in the area of strategic talent management.

This composition is based on a wide range of internationally recognized standard works and references as well as latest discussions found in high-quality human resource and management journals that provide information on the current research of talent management.

2. Talent Management Theory

This chapter presents the theoretical foundation of talent and talent management as well as their integration within the context of the overall business strategy.

2.1 Definition and Concept of Talent and Talent Management

Any discussion and analysis of the topic in question first requires a definition of the basic terms. Notwithstanding the usual problem to find a common understanding of the word, talent can generally be defined as "the sum of a person's abilities"[3], meaning his or hers intrinsic characteristics, attitudes, skills, knowledge, intelligence, experience and motivation that allows an individual to perform certain tasks. It also includes his or her ability to learn and develop.[4]

A good definition and precise meaning of TM (= talent management) is even more difficult to formulate. Although most organizations regularly perform talent management activities, there is no consistent definition of the term as quite a number of different attributes and approaches can be used to characterize it. However, for the purpose of this assignment, talent management is referred to as "a strategic activity aligned with the firm's business strategy that aims to attract, develop and retain talented employees at each level of the organization"[5]. In other words, a company's strategic talent management planning is closely linked to its business strategy.[6]

At the core of this definition is the employee. By developing and maintaining valuable and rare resources that are hard to imitate in form of human capital, organizations

[3] Hatum, A., Next Generation Talent Management, 2010, p.10.
[4] Cf. Ed. Meifert, M., Strategische Personalentwicklung, 2013, p.219; Hatum, A., Next Generation Talent Management, 2010, p.10; Lewis, R., Heckman, R., Talent management, 2006, p.139-154.
[5] Hatum, A., Next Generation Talent Management, 2010, p.13.
[6] Cf. Ed. Meifert, M., Strategische Personalentwicklung, 2013, p.218; eds. Scullion, H., Collings, D., Global Talent Management, 2011, p.5ff.; Hatum, A., Next Generation Talent Management, 2010, p.10-13; Farndale, E., Scullion, H., Sparrow, P., The role of the corporate HR function in global talent management, 2010, p.161-168; Collings, D., Mellahi, K., Strategic Talent Management, 2009, p.304-313; Armstrong, M., A Handbook of Human Resource Management Practice, 2006, p.389-408; Lewis, R., Heckman, R., Talent management, 2006, p.139-154; Ashton, C., Morton, L., Managing talent for competitive advantage, 2005, p.28-31; Boudreau, J., Ramstad, P., Talentship and the new paradigm for human resource management, 2005, p.17−26.

are able to create a sustainable competitive advantage through the deployment of a talent management strategy that covers critical success factors for the overall business strategy such as talent attraction, development and retention as outlined in figure 1.[7]

Figure 1: Connection between Business and Talent Management Strategy[8]

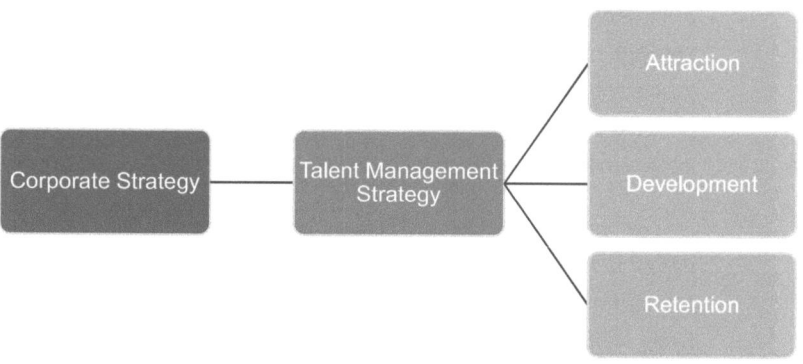

Source: Adapted from Cf. Hatum, A., 2010, p.17

2.2 Talent Management Strategies

This chapter will present the three major talent management strategies of talent attraction, development and retention and derive concrete activities for their organizational implementation.

[7] Cf. Ed. Meifert, M., Strategische Personalentwicklung, 2013, p.218; Hatum, A., Next Generation Talent Management, 2010, p.13-17; Collings, D., Mellahi, K., Strategic Talent Management, 2009, p.304-313; Lewis, R., Heckman, R., Talent management, 2006, p.139-154; Barney, J., Firm Resources and Sustained Competitive Advantage, 1991, p.99-120.
[8] Cf. Hatum, A., Next Generation Talent Management, 2010, p.17.

2.2.1 Attraction

The first step of a successful talent management is attracting the right talent. However, to attract the best candidates, a company should do more than simply analyze its organizational competencies and determine the types of talents required. First, the company requires an attractive EVP (=Employee Value Proposition) as "the set of benefits that characterize .. [the] employer"[9] and enhances the company's reputation as a good place to work at. Second, the company needs to identify appropriate recruitment channels to attract the desired talents and third, it also needs to determine helpful selection practices to identify the right candidates.[10]

2.2.1.1 Employee Value Proposition

An EVP summarizes what employees can expect to receive from the company in exchange for the work they perform. Thus, it can be defined as the "holistic sum of everything people experience and receive while they are part of a company – everything from the intrinsic satisfaction of the work to the environment, leadership, colleagues, compensation and more. It's about how well the company fulfills people's needs, their expectations, and even their dreams"[11].[12]

Generally, an EVP comprises the following set of the company's organizational features and characteristics:[13]

1. Organizational culture (e.g. spirit, risk-taking attitude, corporate social responsibility policy)
2. People (e.g. teamwork, leadership style)

---

[9] Hatum, A., Next Generation Talent Management, 2010, p.37.

[10] Cf. Schuler, R., Jackson, S., Tarique, I., Global talent management and global talent challenges, 2011, p.506-516; eds. Scullion, H., Collings, D., Global Talent Management, 2011, p.26ff.; Hatum, A., Next Generation Talent Management, 2010, p.37f.

[11] Hatum, A., Next Generation Talent Management, 2010, p.38.

[12] Cf. Schuler, R., Jackson, S., Tarique, I., Global talent management and global talent challenges, 2011, p.506-516; Hatum, A., Next Generation Talent Management, 2010, p.38; Guthridge, M., Komm, A., Lawson, E., Making talent a strategic priority, 2008, p.49-59.

[13] Cf. Schuler, R., Jackson, S., Tarique, I., Global talent management and global talent challenges, 2011, p.506-516; Hatum, A., Next Generation Talent Management, 2010, p.38-42; Guthridge, M., Komm, A., Lawson, E., Making talent a strategic priority, 2008, p.49-59.

3. Work characteristics (e.g. innovation, work-life-balance)
4. Rewards (e.g. compensation, incentives)

Figure 2 shows the four sets of characteristics as mentioned above.

Figure 2: Dimensions of Employee Value Proposition[14]

Source: Adapted from Hatum, A., 2010, p.38

An EVP is closely related to employer branding but much more comprehensive as it reflects certain feelings and experiences at the workplace. Thus, it creates an emotional bond which helps the company compete with other companies on the market to attract the best talents.[15]

---

[14] Cf. Hatum, A., Next Generation Talent Management, 2010, p.38.
[15] Cf. Schuler, R., Jackson, S., Tarique, I., Global talent management and global talent challenges, 2011, p.506-516; Hatum, A., Next Generation Talent Management, 2010, p.38-42; Guthridge, M., Komm, A., Lawson, E., Making talent a strategic priority, 2008, p.49-59.

2.2.1.2Recruiting Process

Once the company has created an attractive EVP, it can focus on the next critical step in the talent attraction process, because a strong EVP alone does not ensure that the company will ultimately hire the best candidate.[16]

When attracting the required talents to occupy current vacancies, the company should not only consider internal candidates but also search for additional talent from external in order to be successful. Although the recruitment channels the company chooses to contact potential candidates depends on the target employees, it is important that the different channels used communicate a consistent message that is in line with the reality that the employees face at the company.[17]

There are various innovative trends in the recruitment field that a company can use to identify the right candidates:[18]

- Headhunting
- Employee referrals
- Company website
- Universities/ business schools
- E-recruiting (e.g. Xing, LinkedIn)
- Online simulation tests
- Video résumé and other online channels (e.g. YouTube, blogs)

When talent is scare, companies sometimes have to use multiple channels to ensure attracting the right candidates.[19]

---

[16] Cf. Hatum, A., Next Generation Talent Management, 2010, p.42f.
[17] Cf. eds. Burton-Jones, A., Spender J., Human Capital, 2011, p.318ff.; eds. Scullion, H., Collings, D., Global Talent Management, 2011, p.22f., 105-129; Hatum, A., Next Generation Talent Management, 2010, p.42-45.
[18] Cf. eds. Burton-Jones, A., Spender J., Human Capital, 2011, p.318ff.; Hatum, A., Next Generation Talent Management, 2010, p.48-53.
[19] Cf. eds. Burton-Jones, A., Spender J., Human Capital, 2011, p.318ff.; Hatum, A., Next Generation Talent Management, 2010, p.53.

2.2.1.3 Selection Practices

After the company has decided on the recruiting process, the next step is to determine the selection practices to use. There are several ideas and methods critical to successfully identifying and selecting talent.[20]

To identify and select suitable candidates, the company must align its selection process with its specific organizational needs and consider three different criteria: skills, potential and the extent to which the candidate fits to the company. Determining the kind of talent the company is looking for is an important first step that may indicate which selection practices to use. Moreover, the company must customize its selection criteria (e.g. experience, knowledge, potential, competencies) depending on the position or role of the employee to ensure hiring the right candidate.[21]

The following selection practices can provide a mechanism for filtering the candidates and thus help the company finding the required talents:[22]

- Interviews
- Assessment centers
- Tests (e.g. psychometric tests, attitude tests, personality assessments)
- References

The selection practices a company chooses to use should be the result of deep analysis of the attributes it is looking for in its employees to enable hiring the specific talents required. In addition, the company should not rely on only one method only but use and combine various types to increase the validity of the results and get a clearer picture of a candidate's strengths and abilities.[23]

---

[20] Cf. Hatum, A., Next Generation Talent Management, 2010, p.53f.; Armstrong, M., A Handbook of Human Resource Management Practice, 2006, p.409-438.
[21] Cf. Hatum, A., Next Generation Talent Management, 2010, p.53ff.; Armstrong, M., A Handbook of Human Resource Management Practice, 2006, p.409-438.
[22] Cf. Hatum, A., Next Generation Talent Management, 2010, p.56-62; Armstrong, M., A Handbook of Human Resource Management Practice, 2006, p.409-438.
[23] Cf. Hatum, A., Next Generation Talent Management, 2010, p.61f.; Armstrong, M., A Handbook of Human Resource Management Practice, 2006, p.409-438.

2.2.2 Development

As a result of the company's successful attraction strategy, the second step of talent management is to create a development strategy for both new talents on board and the employees who have been with the organization before.[24]

A company should consider employee development as an integral part of the talent management process. A successful development strategy requires different methods to use for developing different individuals within the organization.[25]

2.2.2.1 Targeting Talent

When targeting talents for development within the organization, it is important to consider that development is different from training. While training focuses on a specific task in the short-term, development focuses on the long-term preparation for dealing with more complex issues. Thus, the company should consider its future business needs to target for development those individuals that will be critical for its future success.[26]

Common targets for development include individuals with high future potential and/or strong past performance. To identify the talents to be targeted for development, the company can apply various or a combination of methods. However, regardless of which method is used, it should include a performance and potential assessment. While the performance assessment focuses on an individual's performance and behavior, the potential assessment analyses a person's advancement potential that requires the ability to manage complex tasks which again is related to the learning

---

[24] Cf. Hatum, A., Next Generation Talent Management, 2010, p.68.
[25] Cf. Hatum, A., Next Generation Talent Management, 2010, p.72.
[26] Cf. Hatum, A., Next Generation Talent Management, 2010, p.74; St. Aubin, D., Carlsen, B., Attract, Engage & Retain Top Talent, 2008, p.175.

capability. With the separate conduction of the performance and potential assessments, the results can be used to determine the targets for development.[27]

Generally, employees that have the greatest expected performance and potential are most likely to contribute to the company's future success whereas the ones with poor expected performance and potential are least likely to contribute. Using a matrix such as presented in figure 3 can help the company to distinguish and categorize its employees.[28]

Figure 3: Performance and Potential Matrix[29]

Performance		Poor	Good	Strong
	Strong	Conundrum	On their way to the top	Stars
	Good	Just a soldier	Average	On their way to the top
	Poor	Out	Nice but useless	Conundrum

Potential

Source: Adapted from Hatum, A., 2010, p.80

---

[27] Cf. Schuler, R., Jackson, S., Tarique, I., Global talent management and global talent challenges, 2011, p.506-516; eds. Scullion, H., Collings, D., Global Talent Management, 2011, p.28f.; Hatum, A., Next Generation Talent Management, 2010, p.74-78; Guthridge, M., Komm, A., Lawson, E., Making talent a strategic priority, 2008, p.49-59; Byham, W., Smith, A., Paese, M., Grow Your Own Leaders, 2002, p.61ff.
[28] Cf. eds. Scullion, H., Collings, D., Global Talent Management, 2011, p.29; Hatum, A., Next Generation Talent Management, 2010, p.78ff.
[29] Cf. Hatum, A., Next Generation Talent Management, 2010, p.80.

Eventually, this matrix can be used to by the company to dig more deeply into each level for establishing clear development decisions and activities.[30]

2.2.2.2 Development Process

When designing an organization's talent development process, it is important to identify which processes and opportunities have the greatest impact when investing in an individual.[31]

In contrast to training and on-the-job experience, the next generation talent management requires a different approach when strategically mapping out individual's development plans. Based on the 80-20 Rule of Pareto, the 19th century Italian sociologist, companies should focus 80% of their development efforts on identifying, assessing and building individual's strengths rather than his or her weaknesses. This strengths-based approach focuses on high valued strengths, meaning strengths that support a better performance on the job in addition to minimum required levels of competency in other required skills.[32]

This analysis provides the basis for the next step of identifying the best development and learning activities to build on individual's strengths. In this context, it is important to consider that over the course of an employee's career, different types of learning and development activities will be used depending on career stage and job responsibility. Such development activities cover three types of learning opportunity: cognitive learning, experience learning and emotional intelligence.[33]

A company has several options for designing specific development plans around these development activities. Besides a structured development program, another attractive option is to use the nine-grid-box presented in the previous chapter to de-

---

[30] Cf. Hatum, A., Next Generation Talent Management, 2010, p.80.
[31] Cf. Hatum, A., Next Generation Talent Management, 2010, p.82.
[32] Cf. Hatum, A., Next Generation Talent Management, 2010, p.82ff.; St. Aubin, D., Carlsen, B., Attract, Engage & Retain Top Talent, 2008, p.175.
[33] Cf. Hatum, A., Next Generation Talent Management, 2010, p.84-89.

termine the appropriate development activities for the different groups within the matrix. Alternatively, the company may also prepare a specific development program for "stars". However, regardless of which development program is chosen, the company must customize some of the activities to improve individuals' strengths.[34]

2.2.3 Retention

A good foundation in terms of talent attraction and development is the key to success of the third and last step of talent retention. In fact, the more time and money a company invests in attracting and developing talent, the more important it is to retain this talent to generate a return on this investment and avoid the hidden costs of losing knowledge and experience.[35]

The concept of retention can be defined as "the effort by an employer to keep desirable workers in order to meet business objectives"[36] and includes both tangible and intangible factors. Most retention programs simply focus on offering attractive benefit packages including holiday pay, schedule adjustments and competitive compensation. However, developing truly effective retention practices should focus on more issues than only short-term extrinsic motivations that influence employees' decision to stay or leave but requires a strategic long-term focus.[37]

The model for long-term retention as shown in figure 4 includes three elements:[38]

1. Organizational Identity = Commitment
2. Compensation and Rewards = Recognition
3. Careers and Employability = Engagement

---

[34] Cf. eds. Scullion, H., Collings, D., Global Talent Management, 2011, p.144-156; Hatum, A., Next Generation Talent Management, 2010, p.89; St. Aubin, D., Carlsen, B., Attract, Engage & Retain Top Talent, 2008, p.175f.

[35] Cf. eds. Scullion, H., Collings, D., Global Talent Management, 2011, p.30; Hatum, A., Next Generation Talent Management, 2010, p.91, 97.

[36] Hatum, A., Next Generation Talent Management, 2010, p.97.

[37] Cf. eds. Scullion, H., Collings, D., Global Talent Management, 2011, p.30; Hatum, A., Next Generation Talent Management, 2010, p.97f.

[38] Cf. Hatum, A., Next Generation Talent Management, 2010, p.98; Armstrong, M., A Handbook of Human Resource Management Practice, 2006, p.271-282.

Figure 4: Long-Term Retention Strategy Model[39]

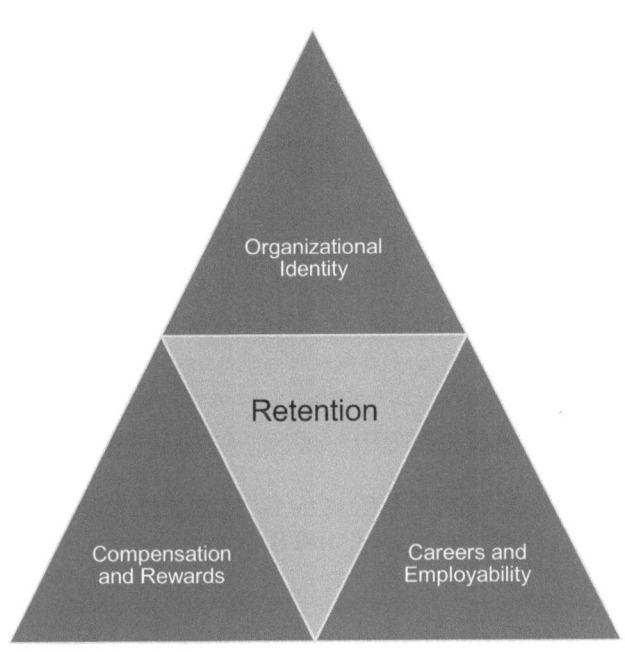

Source: Cf. Hatum, A., 2010, p.98

Together, these three elements contribute to long-term retention by connecting employees to the company through commitment, recognition and engagement.[40]

2.2.3.1 Organizational Identity

The first factor of organizational identity is characterized by three dimensions:[41]

---

[39] Cf. Hatum, A., Next Generation Talent Management, 2010, p.98.

[40] Cf. Hatum, A., Next Generation Talent Management, 2010, p.98; Armstrong, M., A Handbook of Human Resource Management Practice, 2006, p.271-282.

[41] Cf. Hatum, A., Next Generation Talent Management, 2010, p.98.

1. What is considered central to the organization,
2. What makes the organization distinctive,
3. What links the organization's present with its past.

The basis for this definition are the core values of the organization. By defining a set of core values, the company develops a clear identity which allows employees to identify themselves with the organization. While the company's strategy may change as it adapts to new environmental conditions, its identity remains largely unchanged which creates a sense of stability, continuity and coherence among its employees. This coherence in turn creates a sense of commitment towards the organizational core values, mission and beliefs which allows the company to build a strong organizational identity. However, such commitment requires not only writing down the company's vision and mission but the alignment of the theoretical core values with the organizational practice. Especially in times of turmoil, the role of organizational identity is critical to a company's survival as it is the key to a successful retention process.[42]

2.2.3.2Compensation and Rewards

After the company has created a strong identity, the next step in designing a successful retention plan is to connect this process to a transparent and fair system of compensation and rewards to create a sense of recognition among the employees.[43]

Generally, talents can be rewarded for their performance either monetarily or non-monetarily through some other kind of recognition. Accordingly, an organization's compensation and rewards should be used as a party of its retention strategy. Every company has some form of compensation and rewards strategy but in order to establish a successful retention process, it is necessary to go beyond the common compensation practices. To do so, the company must distinguish its employees by segmentation for being able to offer different compensation and rewards to different

---

[42] Cf. Hatum, A., Next Generation Talent Management, 2010, p.98-101.
[43] Cf. eds. Scullion, H., Collings, D., Global Talent Management, 2011, p.29f.; Hatum, A., Next Generation Talent Management, 2010, p.101.

individuals. Such segmentation can be achieved using a performance and potential analysis and matrix as already outlined previously.[44]

When designing compensation and rewards to support a long-time retention strategy, it is important to consider the flexibility as well as the incentives of the system, because a flexible, incentive-based system can adapt compensation and rewards to different types of talent while increasing short- and long-term motivations to stay with the company. Different companies may use different components of a compensation system depending on the possibilities available but generally, a company should follow a performance-related compensation model as shown in figure 5.[45]

Figure 5: Pay-For-Performance Model[46]

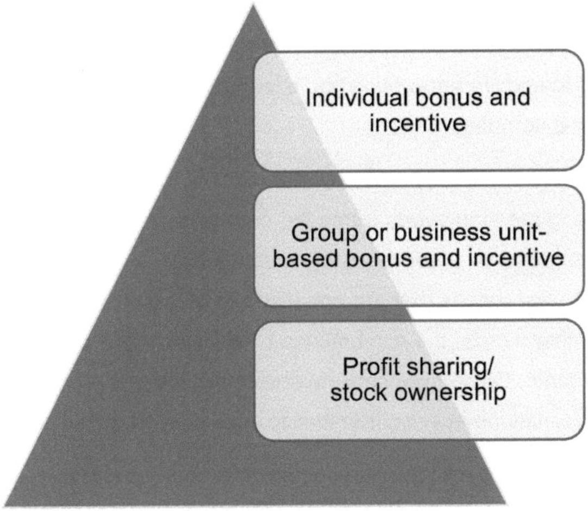

Individual bonus and incentive

Group or business unit-based bonus and incentive

Profit sharing/ stock ownership

Source: Adapted from Hatum, A., 2010, p.106

---

[44] Cf. Schuler, R., Jackson, S., Tarique, I., Global talent management and global talent challenges, 2011, p.506-516; eds. Scullion, H., Collings, D., Global Talent Management, 2011, p.29f.; Hatum, A., Next Generation Talent Management, 2010, p.103f.

[45] Cf. Schuler, R., Jackson, S., Tarique, I., Global talent management and global talent challenges, 2011, p.506-516; eds. Scullion, H., Collings, D., Global Talent Management, 2011, p.29f.; Hatum, A., Next Generation Talent Management, 2010, p.104ff.

[46] Cf. Hatum, A., Next Generation Talent Management, 2010, p.106.

All three levels of performance-related pay should be interconnected and aligned with the organizational strategy.[47]

2.2.3.3 Careers and Employability

As individual's careers and career paths have changed over time and moved away from traditional paradigms, companies are seeking for new career models that create engagement and thus, higher employee retention.[48]

Individual's focus on simply obtaining employment has shifted to employability, which can be defined as "one's relative chances of getting and maintaining different kinds of employment". Instead of simply trying to find a job, individuals are now trying to find the conditions that help them to become and/or remain more marketable. Such conditions can be found in a position that provides continuous learning and development opportunities to be able to meet current market requirements. Thus, opportunities to acquire knowledge and experience are essential for convincing talents to stay with a company.[49]

Under these conditions, a useful concept for companies might be a career portfolio to engage employees within the organization. Just as a financial portfolio, this concept presents a collection of investments in terms of individuals with diverse skills and experiences that are employed to generate some sort of return on investment. In other words, the combination of abilities in the portfolio affects the employability outcome. Companies can implement this concept by offering a wide range of learning and development opportunities to capitalize on employees' skills.[50]

In addition, employees are increasingly looking for flexible career possibilities. Such flexible arrangements for talent retention may include flex-time or part-time jobs and leaves of absence. In this context, a new and successful concept to promote retention might be mass career customization, also referred to as total career customization. This concept refers to the idea of a multiple career path that can be divided into

---

[47] Cf. Hatum, A., Next Generation Talent Management, 2010, p.106.
[48] Cf. Hatum, A., Next Generation Talent Management, 2010, p.107.
[49] Cf. Hatum, A., Next Generation Talent Management, 2010, p.108f.
[50] Cf. Hatum, A., Next Generation Talent Management, 2010, p.109.

the four dimensions of pace, workload, location and role which an employee can adapt according to his or hers individual preferences. Thus, this alternative concept increases flexibility while enabling to follow a long-term career perspective to high-potential employees as well as great performers. Such flexible arrangements that are aligned with a long-term career plan present a great chance of successful retention.[51]

---

[51] Cf. Hatum, A., Next Generation Talent Management, 2010, p.110.

3. Closing

This last chapter provides a summary and conclusion of the main findings as well as an outlook on the future development.

3.1 Summary

In summary, the assignment has presented the definition and concept of talent management in theory and outlined clear implications for organizational practice regarding the three different theoretical talent management strategies of talent attraction, development and retention.

Regarding the first step of talent attraction, the assignment has outlined the importance of an attractive EVP for the company as well as appropriate recruitment channels and helpful selection practices to identify the right candidates.

On the basis of the successful attraction strategy, the assignment has continued with the second step of talent development by outlining how to target talent for development on the basis of their past performance and future potential as well as how to map development by building on individual's strengths.

Concerning the third and last step of talent retention, the assignment has analyzed how to develop effective long-term retention practices to retain the talent that has been attracted and developed using the three elements of organizational identity, flexible compensation and rewards as well as career paths and employability in order to connect employees to the company through commitment, recognition and engagement.

3.2 Conclusion

Coming to a conclusion, the assignment has outlined that a successful talent management strategy including talent attraction, development and retention is able to cover critical success factors for the overall business strategy and enables organizations to create a sustainable competitive advantage by developing and maintaining valuable and rare resources that are hard to imitate.[52]

However, for a talent management strategy to be successful, the three different elements of attraction, development and retention should not be regarded separately but are closely connected and interrelated which is critical for the coherence of the entire process and thus, the performance of the company. In addition, it is important to ensure internal consistency and coherence between the three talent management elements and its practices in order to align the process with the company's overall business strategy and corporate culture while focusing on a long-term perspective.[53]

3.3 Future Outlook

Providing a future outlook on the topic of talent management, it can be said that successful talent management still presents a great challenge to many organizations, often resulting in failures. The response to this is challenge is either to do nothing, means to simply ignore the importance and process of talent management or rely on traditional and outdated approaches, which leads to inconsistencies within the talent management process. This is to say that organizations often find a lack of connections between the different areas for example, some organizations may focus only on attracting and retaining people, overlooking the critical process of development or still overestimate the extent of extrinsic incentives such as pay, and underestimate the increasing role on intrinsic motivation in the context of employee retention. Both scenarios present a risk to the competitive advantage and success of the company and thus, room for future improvement.[54]

---

[52] Cf. Hatum, A., Next Generation Talent Management, 2010, p.124-129; Barney, J., Firm Resources and Sustained Competitive Advantage, 1991, p.99-120.
[53] Cf. Hatum, A., Next Generation Talent Management, 2010, p.124-129.
[54] Cf. Hatum, A., Next Generation Talent Management, 2010, p.124-129; Cappelli, P., Talent Management for the Twenty-First Century, 2008, p.1-9; Barney, J., Firm Resources and Sustained Competitive Advantage, 1991, p.99-120.

Bibliography

Armstrong, Michael (A Handbook of Human Resource Management Practice, 2006): A Handbook of Human Resource Management Practice, 10th edition, London: Kogan Page, 2006

Byham, William C., Smith, Audrey B., Paese, Matthew J. (Grow Your Own Leaders, 2002): Grow Your Own Leaders: How to Identify, Develop, and Retain Leadership Talent, New York: Financial Times Prentice Hall, 2002

Burton-Jones, Alan, Spender J. C. (Eds.) (Human Capital, 2011): Human Capital, Oxford: Oxford University Press, 2011

Cappelli, Peter (Talent on Demand, 2008): Talent on Demand: Managing Talent in an Age of Uncertainty, Boston: Harvard Business Press, 2008

Hatum, Andrés (Next Generation Talent Management, 2010): Next Generation Talent Management – Talent Management to Survive Turmoil, Hampshire: Palgrave Macmillan, 2010

Heidelberger, Michael, Kornherr, Lothar (Eds.) (Handbuch der Personalberatung, 2014): Handbuch der Personalberatung – Konzepte, Prozesse und Visionen, 2nd edition, München: Vahlen, 2014

Meifert, Matthias T. (Ed.) (Strategische Personalentwicklung, 2013): Strategische Personalentwicklung – Ein Programm in acht Etappen, 3rd edition, Wiesbaden: Springer Gabler, 2013

Michaels, Ed, Handfield-Jones, Helen, Axelrod, Beth (The War for Talent, 2001): The War for Talent, Boston: Harvard Business School Press, 2001

Scullion, Hugh, Collings, David G. (Eds.) (Global Talent Management, 2011): Global Talent Management, New York: Routledge, 2011

St. Aubin, Donna, Carlsen, Brian J. (Attract, Engage & Retain Top Talent, 2008): Attract, Engage & Retain Top Talent: 50 Plus One Strategies Used by the Best, Bloomington: Author House, 2008

Ashton, Chris, Morton, Lynne (Managing talent for competitive advantage, 2005): Managing talent for competitive advantage: Taking a systemic approach to talent management, in: Strategic HR Review, Vol.4, No.5, p.28-31

Barney, Jay, (Firm Resources and Sustained Competitive Advantage, 1991): Firm Resources and Sustained Competitive Advantage, in: Journal of Management, Vol.17, No.1, p.99-120

Beechler, Schon, Woodward, Ian C. (The global "war for talent", 2009): The global "war for talent", in: Journal of International Management, Vol.15, p.273-285

Boudreau, John W., Ramstad, Peter M. (Talentship and the new paradigm for human resource management, 2005): Talentship and the new paradigm for human resource management: From professional practice to strategic talent decision science, in: Human Resource Planning, Vol.28, No.2, p.17–26

Cappelli, Peter (Talent Management for the Twenty-First Century, 2008): Talent Management for the Twenty-First Century, in: Harvard Business Review, Reprint R0803E, p.1-9

Collings, David G., Mellahi, Kamel (Strategic Talent Management, 2009): Strategic Talent Management: A review and research agenda, in: Human Resource Management Review, Vol.19, No.4, p.304-313

Farndale, Elaine, Scullion, Hugh, Sparrow, Paul (The role of the corporate HR function in global talent management, 2010): The role of the corporate HR function in global talent management, in: Journal of World Business, Vol.45, p.161-168

Guthridge, Matthew, Komm, Asmus B., Lawson, Emily (Making talent a strategic priority, 2008): Making talent a strategic priority, in: The McKinsey Quarterly, Vol.1, p.49-59

Lewis, Robert E., Heckman, Robert J. (Talent management, 2006): Talent management: A critical review, in: Human Resource Management Review, Vol.16, p.139-154

Schuler, Randall S., Jackson, Susan E., Tarique, Ibraiz (Global talent management and global talent challenges, 2011): Global talent management and global talent challenges: Strategic opportunities for IHRM, in: Journal of World Business, Vol.46, p.506-516

ITM-Checklist

Topics	The sine qua non of success	Comments/Suggestions
Economics	Which macroeconomic relevance is inherent in the topics?	In the economics area, it is important to consider the impact of economic forces that shape the environment a company operates in, particularly including the employment market.
Marketing	Which advantages and disadvantages arise out of the suggestions for marketing measures, external impact, and the company's general productivity? Which measures should be taken concerning internal and/or external marketing?	In the area of marketing, it is important to consider that marketing activities can also be used to promote the company itself in terms of employer branding and creating a distinctive Employee Value Proposition for a successful attraction of talents.
Human Resource Management	Which personnel consequences (quantitative or qualitative) result from the suggestions?	With regard to human resources, conclusions can be drawn on the changing role of the Human Resource department and its activities within an organization.

Corporate Finance	What criteria have to be considered when choosing appropriate terms of financing? Which risks are existing and what kind of coverage is suggested? How should the influence of external factors be evaluated?	Corporate finance particularly deals with the analysis of the costs that derive from attracting and developing talent. The more time and money a company invests in talent attraction and development, the more important it is to retain this talent to generate a return on this investment and avoid the hidden costs of losing knowledge and experience.
Strategic Corporate Management	How is the topic's strategic relevance to be evaluated, especially concerning the aspects of securing existence, competitive advantages, tying up resources, sustainability, and risks?	Strategic management involves considering the increasing strategic focus of organizational talent management planning as well the need for its close connection and alignment to the overall business strategy.
Business Law	Which legal fields are affected by the suggestions? What has to be arranged in order to create legal security from the company's point of view?	In the area of business law, changes within the business environment and emerging trends of talent management should be considered for policy-making purpose within the organization.

Soft Skills & Leadership Qualities	Which demands does the realization of the suggestions require of the responsible managers? What leadership behavior is expedient?	Regarding soft skills and leadership qualities, it is important to consider that especially in the context of talent development, companies should also focus on learning activities that enhance individuals' soft skills and emotional intelligence.
Research Methods	What sources of information should be practiced in order to stay up to date in the field of topics?	In the research methods area, the company can use different recruitment channels to attract the right talent. Moreover, employee surveys should be undertaken regularly to enhance talent retention.
Management Decision Making	Which decision criteria should be practiced on the choice of alternatives?	In management decision-making, it is important to consider that talent decisions may have critical consequences for an organization. There are several ideas and methods critical to successfully identifying and selecting talent which is why the company has to carefully determine appropriate selection

		practices to identify the right candidates.
Business Ethics and Sustainability	What relevant ethical question may arise in the given context? Which management measures could be useful to address these potential challenges effectively and efficiently? Which sustainability challenges may occur in the given context?	In business ethics and sustainability, it should be considered that ethical standards as well as ecological and social responsibility as part of the corporate culture may present a distinctive employee value proposition that influences talent attraction and retention.